God bless you! Rejoice!

Presented to

Lisa Cole

On the occasion of

P.E. 21

From

Laura Easey

Date

Oct 2000

Barbour Publishing, Inc. expresses its appreciation to those who generously gave permission to reprint copyrighted material. Diligent effort has been made to identify, locate, contact, and secure permission to use copyrighted material. If any permissions or acknowledgments have been inadvertently omitted or if such permissions were not received by the time of publication, the publisher would sincerely appreciate receiving complete information so that correct credit can be given in future editions. "One Easter" by Sharon Banigan. Taken from *Prayers and Graces: Dennis the Menace* by Hank Ketcham. Published by Westminster/John Knox Press, Louisville, KY 40202.

ISBN 1-57748-762-1

All Scripture quotations (unless otherwise noted) are taken from the King James Version of the Bible.

Scripture quotations marked NIV are taken from the HOLY BIBLE, NEW INTERNATIONAL VERSION®, NIV®, © 1973, 1978, 1984 by the International Bible Society. Used by permission of Zondervan Publishing House. All rights reserved.

Published by Barbour Publishing, Inc., P.O. Box 719 Uhrichsville, Ohio 44683
http://www.barbourbooks.com

ecpa Member of the
Evangelical Christian
Publishers Association

Printed in China.

WHEN LOVE CONQUERED ALL

Celebrating the Resurrection of Christ

Bonnie Harvey

BARBOUR
PUBLISHING, INC.

"He is risen, indeed!"

The joyous conviction expressed in this greeting—once exchanged by the early Christians—reverberates today. Because the Resurrection is the very embodiment of our hope, the Easter season is the highlight of the Christian calendar.

The Resurrection established that Jesus is the Son of God: the fulfillment of all prophecy, the Sacrifice for all sin, and the King for all eternity.

As this significant season approaches, spend some time in silent reflection and prayer.

Then. . .sense the awe. Anticipate the hope. Experience the joy.

PREPARATION

How lovely is your dwelling place,
   O LORD Almighty!
My soul yearns, even faints
   for the courts of the LORD;
my heart and my flesh cry out
   for the living God.

PSALM 84:1–2, NIV

The dauntless crocuses poke their emerald tips through the last of the winter's snows, and the saffron daffodils sway in the chilly breeze. Glorious forsythia bushes dot the greening lawns, and bold tulips splash their varied colors in carefully tended beds. Rosebush stems bulge with the promise of their first buds. After the long dreariness of winter, our spirits are refreshed by the kaleidoscope of colors displayed among the spring flowers. Yet for the gardener—more than anyone else—this time has unusual significance. The gardener has planted, cultivated, and nurtured, and now waits expectantly for the first signs of life. The enjoyment derived depends upon the effort expended.

And so it is with the enjoyment of the Easter season. While Easter is an "internal," or spiritual, holiday, external preparation can enhance our internal appreciation. Special seasonal activities with our families, a few pertinent read-aloud stories, and discussions that clarify the traditions we follow can quicken our spirits to perceive the true meaning of Easter in a refreshing way.

ACTIVITY TIME

As Passion Week, or Holy Week, begins, the family can be involved in this activity to focus their minds on the real meaning of Easter. On small slips of paper, write Scripture references (one reference per slip) that correspond to each day's event throughout Holy Week. Place each slip in a plastic Easter egg, and place the eggs in a decorated basket. Just before or after a meal together, members can take turns selecting an egg and reading aloud the designated verses.

Some Suggested Verses:

Palm Sunday: Preparation for Jerusalem entry—Matthew 21:1–9
Protest by the Pharisees—Luke 19:37–40
Triumphal entry into Jerusalem—Matthew 21:10–16
Return to Bethany—Matthew 21:17

Monday: The fig tree cursed—Mark 11:13–14
Cleansing of the Temple—Mark 11:15–17
The plot against Jesus—Luke 19:47–48
Jesus outside the city—Luke 21:37–38

Tuesday:	The withered fig tree—Mark 11:20–22
	Jesus and John the Baptist—Luke 7:19–29
	The widow's mites—Luke 21:1–4
	A resurrection question—Mark 12:18–27
	The Great Commandment—Matthew 22:34–40
Wednesday:	The chief priests—Matthew 26:1–5
	The alabaster box—Matthew 26:6–13
	Judas' Betrayal, three accounts—
	Matthew 26:14–16
	Mark 14:10–11
	John 13:1–2
Thursday:	Preparation for Passover, three accounts—
	Matthew 26:17–19
	Mark 14:12–16
	Luke 22:7–13
Friday:	The Disciples—Matthew 26:20–35
	The Garden—Matthew 26:36–56
	Religious Trial—Matthew 26:57–27:2
	Roman Trial—Matthew 27:11–31
	Peter's Denial—John 18:15–27
Saturday:	The Crucifixion, four accounts—
	Matthew 27:32–66
	Mark 15:15–47

WHEN LOVE CONQUERED ALL

Luke 23:27–56
John 19:23–42

Sunday: The Resurrection, four accounts—
Matthew 28:1–20
Mark 16:1–18
Luke 24:1–51
John 20:1–19

Other Activities for Families this Week:

• Watch a video on the life of Jesus
• Attend a passion play
• Attend an Easter sunrise service
• Attend an Easter concert
• Read aloud the poems and stories included in this book
• Sing selected hymns together at home each day, focusing on selected themes, such as: The Birth of Jesus; Jesus and Me; Worshipping the Lord; The Sacrifice of Praise; Spreading the Good News; The Glory of the Cross; Following Jesus; He is Risen!

Jessie's Easter Bonnet

No point in saying anything to Mother, thought Jessie dismally. *I know if she could, she would probably buy me the frilly, pink-and-white hat in Arenson's display window, but we simply can't afford it.*

Jessie's mom, Alice, was a widow with three children besides Jessie to feed and clothe. But that fact didn't stop the yearning in ten-year-old Jessie's heart. If only once she could have some new clothes like the other kids instead of "make-do's" and "hand-me-downs"! She knew that her best friend Sally had already bought a beautiful blue-and-white dress for Easter. And Sally's grandmother was buying her a hat and shoes to match.

"Jessie, why are you so quiet?" Alice asked her.

"Well. . .I was thinking about the beautiful hat in Arenson's window. . ." Jessie's voice trailed away.

"Oh, Jessie, I'm sorry we can't get it for you. The twins need new shoes."

Later that day as Jessie stood outside Arenson's admiring "her" hat, Mr. Arenson stepped outside. "Something in the window catch your eye?"

Jessie nodded shyly, then hesitatingly, and with a longing that surprised her, she pointed to the beribboned hat. "That hat over there. I think it's the most beautiful one I've ever seen!"

"You're Alice Simpson's little girl, aren't you?"

"Yes sir," she replied politely.

"Your mother's a mighty fine woman. I know it's been hard on her these past four years since your daddy's been gone. Hmm," said Mr. Arenson, "I need to check on something. Wait right here, would you?"

A few minutes later, he returned carrying a big square box. "Here, this is for you," he said, handing it to her. "But don't open it 'til you get home."

Jessie breathed a whispery, surprised thanks, then carefully walked down the street, anxious to get home and open the box.

"Look, Mom," she called, coming in the back door. "Mr. Arenson gave me this box." Deftly she unwrapped it and looked inside. There, in all of its pink-and-white Easter finery, was a hat exactly like the one in the window!

"Ooooh, Mom, look! It's the hat I wanted! How good of Mr. Arenson to give it to me! I must go back and thank him again at once!"

Although Jessie attended church that Easter Sunday wearing last year's slightly faded dress, no one noticed. They were too busy admiring the beaming face under the lovely pink-and-white hat. That was the happiest Easter Jessie could ever remember.

The Joy of Easter

Excitement glowed on Linda's eager face. "Hurry up, Robert, or we'll be late for the service!"

Robert, still rubbing sleep from his light-blue eyes, cautiously made his way to the living room. It was already 5:15, and the sunrise service, atop a nearby mountain, was scheduled to start at 6:00.

"I finally found my cuff link. Let's go, Linda. We haven't any time to lose."

As the two settled into their old Mercury, a shiver ran down Linda's spine. The cool springtime air rushed past the car. Outside the window, though not yet visible in the early morning shadows, she could picture the blooming yellow daffodils and the budding dogwood trees.

"Oh Robert, isn't it wonderful to know the Lord—and to know He lives inside of us?"

Robert nodded his agreement, adding, "What a difference Jesus has made in our lives! The peace and love and joy He has brought to us is beyond words! Linda, He has transformed our marriage!"

"I know. I'm so glad we know Him." Within a short time, Linda and Robert worshipped the Lord at their first Easter sunrise service. They had come to know Him only three short months earlier, but they knew Jesus was alive—He was alive within their hearts.

TRADITIONS
OF THE SEASON

Traditions, in and of themselves, are not necessarily something to adhere to—or abandon. Often traditions are the equivalent of "We've always done it this way," and sometimes nobody can even recall why it was done in that particular fashion initially. The Easter season is rich in tradition, and while the events can be enjoyed even while overlooking many traditions, the observance of those traditions, coupled with the understanding of them, can enrich our commemorative experience.

Shrove Tuesday

The tradition actually begins on the last day before the Lenten season, Shrove Tuesday. Traditionally this was the day Christians went to confession and were "shriven," or absolved from their sins. (The word "shrove" is a form of "shriven.") We, however, can come to Jesus directly every day, confess our sins, and receive His forgiveness. We need not wait for "Shrove Tuesday"!

> Search me, O God, and know my heart:
> try me, and know my thoughts:
> And see if there be any wicked way in me,
> and lead me in the way everlasting.
>
> Psalm 139:23–24

> If we confess our sins,
> he is faithful and just to forgive us our sins,
> and to cleanse us from all unrighteousness.
>
> 1 John 1:9

Because Shrove Tuesday was also the last opportunity for merrymaking and indulgence in food and drink before the austere Lenten period, it gained the appellation of "Fat Tuesday." From other customs of making donuts or pancakes on this day, it is also informally called "Donut Day" or "Pancake Day."

The pancake was likely one bread which the housewife of Jesus' time loved, since it was quick, filling, and economical. She may have baked hers on a hot stone; some housewives, no doubt, used a hole dug in the ground for their oven. In this, the sides were smoothly plastered and the fire was placed in the bottom. When it was sufficiently heated, the bread or cake was placed on the smooth sides and baked swiftly.

The Season of Lent

From before the foundations of the world, Jesus was preparing for what would happen in the last few days of his life. That we prepare ourselves for the remembrance of this significant season is only fitting. The days during which we give particular attention to preparation for Easter—a forty-day period beginning with Ash Wednesday and extending, with the omission of Sundays, to the day before Easter—is called the Lenten season. Of the Sundays of Lent, the first is Passion Sunday, and the last is Palm Sunday. The week preceding Easter, including Good Friday, is Holy Week. Lent ends at midnight on the Saturday before Easter Sunday.

Observed as a time of penitence, abstinence, and fasting, Lent began early in Church history to commemorate Christ's forty-day fast in the wilderness. The word "Lent" simply means "springtime," and has varying traditions associated with it.

The early Christians used the Lenten season as a time for instruction of new converts which culminated in their pre-Easter baptism. Thus it was both a time of learning about the Christian faith as well as a time of moral examination and soul-searching.

This time of self-examination can take place between a Christian and the Lord and consists of humbling oneself before Him, of praying, and of various kinds of fasting. The apostle Paul admonishes us to "Examine yourselves, whether ye be in the faith" (2 Corinthians 13:5).

Ash Wednesday

Lent commences with Ash Wednesday, so named from the ceremonial use of ashes as a symbol of penitence. The custom in some churches is for the priest, after prayer, to take ashes and make the sign of the Cross on a believer's forehead.

Although many Protestant churches do not practice this custom, the accompanying command can nevertheless be taken to heart:

> "Remember, man, that thou art dust and
> unto dust thou shalt return."

Fasting

Because the general concept of fasting is too vast a subject to cover here, only fasting as it relates to Lent will be discussed. Fasting could be defined broadly as "self-denial." The range of interpretation varies: denying one's self food, whether skipping a meal (or several meals) or choosing not to eat a favorite food, can be considered fasting. Of course, the gamut of reasons for fasting reaches from humbling one's self to bringing more discipline into one's life. Although in general fasting the participants can be an individual or a nation, Lenten fasting is focused on the individual to engender personal spiritual introspection and a closer relationship with God.

> Precious Savior, why do I fear your scrutiny? Yours is an examen of love. Still, I am afraid. . .afraid of what may surface. Even so, I invite you to search me to the depths so that I may know myself—and You—in fuller measure. Amen.
>
> —Richard J. Foster

The most important aspect of fasting is the heart motive. Once this spiritual discipline is chosen, it needs to be practiced as unto the Lord. The classic scriptural passage concerning fasting is found in Isaiah 58. Early in this chapter, God says to His people: "Behold, in the day of your fast ye find pleasure." Then He describes the fast that He delights in:

Is not this the fast that I have chosen?
to loose the bands of wickedness, to
undo the heavy burdens, and to let the
oppressed go free, and that ye break every yoke?
Is it not to deal thy bread to the hungry,
and that thou bring the poor that are cast
out to thy house? when thou seest the
naked, that thou cover him; and that
thou hide not thyself from thine own flesh?
Then shall thy light break forth as the
morning, and thine health shall spring forth
speedily: and thy righteousness shall go
before thee; the glory of the LORD shall be thy rereward.
Then shalt thou call, and the LORD shall
answer; thou shalt cry, and he shall say, Here I am.

Isaiah 58:6–9

John Wesley and the early Methodists disciplined themselves to fast every Friday. While the timing does not relate to Lent, some of Wesley's insight on the subject of fasting, summarized in the well-known Sermon 27, is beneficial:

First, let it be done unto the Lord, with our eye singly fixed on Him. Let our intention herein be this, and this alone, to glorify our Father which

is in heaven; to express our sorrow and shame for our manifold transgressions of His holy law; to wait for an increase of purifying grace,
drawing our affections to things above; to add seriousness and earnest-
ness to our prayers; to avert the wrath of God; and to obtain all the great
and precious promises which He hath made to us in Jesus Christ. . . .
Fasting is only a way which God hath ordained, wherein we wait for
His unmerited mercy; and wherein, without any desert of ours, He hath
promised freely to give us His blessing.

Palm Sunday

The crowds widely acclaimed Jesus as He rode into Jerusalem on a donkey. . .
they spread palm branches in His path and cried:

Hosanna to the Son of David! Blessed is he that comes in the name of
the Lord! Hosanna in the highest! (Matthew 21:9, NIV).

Maundy Thursday

Following Jesus' triumphal entry into the city of Jerusalem on Palm Sunday, He continued to teach, preach, and heal. His disciples prepared the Passover meal, as He directed, for Thursday evening. This Thursday is known as Maundy Thursday, the name "Maundy" being derived from the first word in an anthem traditionally sung in a ceremony on that day. In England, a custom survives of giving "maundy pennies" (or alms) to the poor, recalling an earlier practice in which the sovereign washed the feet of the poor on Maundy Thursday. In most European countries, the day is simply known as Holy Thursday.

During Thursday evening, Jesus washed His disciples' feet, broke the bread and poured out the wine.

ACCORDING TO THY GRACIOUS WORD

According to Thy gracious Word,
In meek humility,
This will I do, my dying Lord,
I will remember Thee.

Thy body, broken for my sake,
My bread from heav'n shall be;
Thy testamental cup I take,
And thus remember Thee.

WHEN LOVE CONQUERED ALL

> Gethsemane can I forget?
> Or there Thy conflict see,
> Thine agony and bloody sweat,
> And not remember Thee?
>
> When to the cross I turn mine eyes,
> And rest on Calvary,
> Lamb of God, my Sacrifice,
> I must remember Thee.
>
> —James Montgomery

After the Passover meal, He shared His heart and soul with His followers before offering a prayer for them as recorded in John chapters thirteen to seventeen.

"And now, Father, glorify me in your presence with the glory I had with you before the world began. I have revealed you to those whom you gave me out of the world. . . . For I gave them the words you gave me and they accepted them. They knew with certainty that I came from you, and they believed that you sent me. My prayer is not that you take them out of the world but that you protect them from the evil one. My prayer is not for them alone. I pray also for those who will believe in me through their message" (John 17:5–6, 8, 15, 20, NIV).

In commemoration, the Last Supper, known also as Communion, is commonly served, and the ceremony of the washing of the feet is performed. Participants sometimes wash the feet of twelve people, symbolic of Christ's washing of His disciples' feet.

Following the Passover meal, Jesus went to the Garden of Gethsemane where He prayed, "O my Father, if it be possible, let this cup pass from me: nevertheless not as I will, but as thou wilt" (Matthew 26:39).

Momentarily, Judas arrived with a band of soldiers and kissed Jesus on the cheek—a predetermined gesture of betrayal, and the Roman soldiers took Jesus into custody. During the next several hours, Jesus was tried by a religious court and then by civil courts under Pontius Pilate and King Herod. Pilate expressed reluctance to sentence Jesus because he believed in His innocence, but succumbed when the Jerusalem mob cried, "Crucify Him, crucify Him!"

Good Friday

Jesus was crucified on Friday, the day after Passover. The Jewish priests convicted Him on the charge that He blasphemed God. As a matter of course, two thieves were also put to death on crosses the same day, one on each side of Jesus.

Spring Cleaning

Every year the Jewish people celebrate a feast called Passover to remember how God freed them from slavery and bondage in Egypt. Passover looks back to the lamb whose blood was applied to the door of each house. Because of the lamb's blood on the door, the Lord's death angel "passed over" the people inside.

Then for seven days following Passover, every Jewish household was to be totally free from leaven, which represented sin. So the whole family got busy and cleaned every square inch of their home! Apparently, to them we owe the tradition of spring cleaning, although the process in Christian circles carries no spiritual connotations.

Because the blood of Jesus Christ the Lamb is applied to a believer's heart and life, the penalty of sin will not come upon him. And certainly every square inch of the believer's heart should be cleaned from the leaven of sin as he is being conformed to the likeness of Christ.

The Date of Easter

The dates for Easter (the Resurrection of Christ) and the Jewish Passover coincided in the first century: since Judaism's calendar was based on the lunar cycle, both events followed the first full moon in the Spring. Much conflict resulted from both celebrations being held at the same time. The Christians wanted to begin a week-long celebration of Christ's Resurrection, and they wished to have it begin on Sunday, but Passover does not fall on any particular weekday.

Constantine the Great summoned the famous Council of Nicaea in A.D. 325 to resolve the date of Easter—and all the anxiety the churches had over it! It was decided that Easter must be celebrated everywhere on the same day and that this day must be a Sunday. It was further decided that to avoid any coincidental celebration, it must be the first Sunday after the full moon following the vernal equinox, March 21, with one reservation. The English prayer book states: "If the full moon happens upon a Sunday, Easter-day is the Sunday after."

New Clothes

The custom of new clothes for Easter began when the early Christian converts were baptized the day before Easter. After their baptism, they put on new clothing to show their new life in Christ!

New clothes are exciting and they give us an emotional lift, but we should always remember how this tradition began and celebrate our inner life in Christ more than our outward display of new clothes!

MEDITATION

Where there is charity and wisdom, there is neither fear
nor ignorance. Where there is patience and humility,
there is neither anger nor vexation. Where there is poverty
and joy, there is neither greed nor avarice.
Where there is peace and meditation,
there is neither anxiety nor doubt.
—St. Francis of Assisi

The specific purpose of our preparation is the benefit and blessing that can be ours through contemplation of the events surrounding the days preceding and including Easter. As we now ponder the significance of His humility in becoming human, His submission to the will of His Father, His suffering for our sin, and His redemption of mankind, may the love in our hearts erupt into expressions of praise and adoration to Him.

Jesus was chosen before the foundations of the world to come to earth as a tiny baby born in Bethlehem. He Who is "Wonderful, Counsellor, The mighty God, The everlasting Father, The Prince of Peace" willingly came not only in the form of a man but as a totally helpless infant.

Then, not only as an infant, but to the poorest of the poor, in the lowest of the lowliest. "And she [Mary] brought forth her firstborn son, and wrapped him in swaddling clothes, and laid him in a manger; because there was no room for them in the inn" (Luke 2:7).

WHEN LOVE CONQUERED ALL

Who, being in very nature God, did not consider equality with God something to be grasped, but made himself nothing, taking the very nature of a servant, being made in human likeness. And being found in appearance as a man, he humbled himself and became obedient to death—even death on a cross!

Philippians 2:6–9, NIV

Jesus counted the cost of coming to this world, knowing that He "came not to be ministered unto, but to minister, and to give his life a ransom for many" (Matthew 20:28). Still, He deliberately came to give "himself for us an offering and a sacrifice to God for a sweetsmelling savour" (Ephesians 5:2), and did not swerve from His purpose. He set His face like a flint to do His Father's will. Following His baptism in the River Jordan by John the Baptist, Jesus was led by the Holy Spirit into the wilderness for forty days where He prayed and fasted. Afterward, He endured Satan's temptations, which centered around: 1) Food 2) Power, and 3) Wealth and Fame. To each of these temptations, Jesus responded with scripture.

In response to the temptation to "turn the stones into bread," Jesus told Satan: "Man shall not live by bread alone, but by every word that proceedeth out of the mouth of God." Next the Devil challenged, "If thou be the Son of God, cast thyself down: for it is written, He shall give his angels charge concerning thee: and in their hands they shall bear thee up, lest at any time thou dash thy foot against a stone." Jesus told him, "It is written again, Thou shalt not tempt the Lord thy God." To the last temptation, when the Devil set Jesus on a high mountain and showed Him the kingdoms of the world, offering to give them to Him in return for His worship, Jesus responded, "Get thee hence, Satan: for it is written, Thou shalt worship the Lord thy God, and him only shalt thou serve" (Matthew 4:1–10).

Almost immediately, Jesus began to preach saying, "Repent: for the kingdom of heaven is at hand." As He walked near the Sea of Galilee, Jesus saw two fishermen, Peter and Andrew. He called them to become His disciples and follow Him. Ultimately, Jesus gathered twelve disciples, calling them to leave everything and follow Him. "And He said to them all, If any man will come after me, let him deny himself, and take up his cross daily, and follow me" (Luke 9:23).

What He asked of His disciples was no less than what He Himself was doing. He continually was denying Himself and carrying His cross. No one diverted his attention from His mission. "When the time was come that he should be received up, he stedfastly set his face to go to Jerusalem" (Luke 9:51).

He was despised and rejected by men, a man of sorrows, and familiar with suffering. . . . Surely he took up our infirmities and carried our sorrows, yet we considered him stricken by God, smitten by him, and afflicted. But he was pierced for our transgressions, he was crushed for our iniquities; the punishment that brought us peace was upon him, and by his wounds we are healed (Isaiah 53:3–5, NIV).

Continuing this time of meditation, let's reflect on the death Jesus endured for us on the Cross. Salvation is free to us, but it was not free to Jesus Christ. He suffered unspeakable torture and agony as He paid the penalty of our sins and opened the way for us to enter heaven. Charles Spurgeon had the following thoughts concerning the meaning of the Cross:

> In the cross of Christ we glory, because we regard it as a matchless exhibition of the attributes of God. . . . In the cross we see a strange conjunction of what once appeared to be two opposite qualities—justice and mercy. . . . We can never tell which of the attributes of God shines most glorious in the sacrifice of Christ; they each one find a glorious high throne in the person and work of the Lamb of God, that taketh away the sin of the world. Since it has become, as it were, the disc which reflects the character and perfections of God, it is meet that we should glory in the cross of Christ, and none shall stay us of our boasting.

But God forbid that I should glory, save in the cross of our Lord Jesus Christ, by whom the world is crucified unto me, and I unto the world (Galatians 6:14).

When I Survey the Wondrous Cross

When I survey the wondrous cross,
On which the Prince of glory died,
My richest gain I count but loss,
And pour contempt on all my pride.

Forbid it, Lord, that I should boast,
Save in the death of Christ, my God;
All the vain things that charm me most,
I sacrifice them to His blood.

. . . .

Were the whole realm of nature mine,
That were a present far too small;
Love so amazing, so divine,
Demands my soul, my life, my all.

—Isaac Watts

Granted, the Cross is a gruesome instrument of ignominious death, but we see glory shining through it because of its effect upon our lives. Jesus has invited whosoever will to come and experience the life-changing, purifying impact of His finished work upon the Cross. Whosoever will. Think on it! Regardless of our status in life, our past, our characteristics, or our abilities, the requirement of redemption has been fully satisfied. Nothing remains for us to do but to accept for ourselves the forgiveness of our sins. Only our own refusal to come can exclude us from the blessings of His grace.

A Prayer of Petition

Almighty and everlasting God, who hatest nothing that thou hast made, and dost forgive the sins of all those who are penitent; Create and make in us new and contrite hearts, that we, worthily lamenting our sins and acknowledging our wretchedness, may obtain of thee, the God of all mercy, perfect remission and forgiveness; through Jesus Christ our Lord. Amen.

Book of Common Prayer

Whosoever Will

"Whosoever heareth," shout, shout the sound!
Spread the blessed tidings all the world around;
Spread the joyful news wherever man is found;
"Whosoever will may come."

Whosoever cometh need not delay,
Now the door is open, enter while you may;
Jesus is the true, the only Living Way;
"Whosoever will may come."

REFRAIN
"Whosoever will, whosoever will,"
Send the proclamtion over vale and hill;
'Tis a loving father, calls the wanderer home:
"Whosoever will may come."

—P. P. Bliss

CELEBRATION

I pray also that the eyes of your heart may be enlightened in order that you may know the hope to which he has called you, the riches of his glorious inheritance in the saints, and his incomparably great power for us who believe. That power is like the working of his mighty strength, which he exerted in Christ when he raised him from the dead and seated him at his right hand in the heavenly realms (Ephesians 1:18–20, NIV).

Were You There?

Were you there when they crucified my Lord?
Were you there when they crucified my Lord?
    Were you there when they nailed Him to the tree?
    Were you there when they nailed Him to the tree?
Were you there when they pierced Him in the side?
Were you there when they pierced Him in the side?
    Were you there when the sun refused to shine?
    Were you there when the sun refused to shine?
Were you there when they laid Him in the tomb?
Were you there when they laid Him in the tomb?

CHORUS
Oh! Sometimes it causes me to tremble, tremble, tremble,
Were you there when they crucified my Lord?

Were you there when He rose up from the grave?
Were you there when He rose up from the grave?

CHORUS
Oh! Sometimes I feel like shouting, Glory! Glory! Glory!
Were you there when He rose up from the grave?

CHRIST IS RISEN!
HE IS RISEN INDEED!

The first day of the week cometh Mary Magdalene early, when it was yet dark, unto the sepulchre, and seeth the stone taken away from the sepulchre. . . . And they [the angels] say unto her, Woman, why weepest thou? She saith unto them, Because they have taken away my Lord, and I know not where they have laid him. And when she had thus said, she turned herself back, and saw Jesus standing, and knew not that it was Jesus. . . . Jesus saith unto her, Mary. She turned herself, and saith unto him, Rabboni; which is to say, Master (John 20:1, 13–16).

One Easter

Joyfully, this Easter day,
I kneel, a little child, to pray;
Jesus, who hath conquered death,
Teach me, with my every breath,
To praise and worship Thee.
　　　　　　　　—Sharon Banigan

Although many have attempted to discredit the Resurrection, it has been authenticated by many witnesses including Matthew, Mark, John, and others enumerated by the apostle Paul.

> For I delivered unto you first of all that which I also received, how that Christ died for our sins according to the scriptures; And that he was buried, and that he rose again the third day according to the scriptures: And that he was seen of Cephas, then of the twelve: After that, he was seen of above five hundred brethren at once; of whom the greater part remain unto this present, but some are fallen asleep. After that, he was seen of James; then of all the apostles. And last of all he was seen of me also, as of one born out of due time.
>
> 1 Corinthians 15:3–8

Because people in the days of Paul were saying Christ had not risen from the dead, he refuted their arguments by following the premise to its logical end: "But if there be no resurrection of the dead, then is Christ not risen: . . .then is our preaching vain, and your faith is also vain. . . . Ye are yet in your sins" (1 Corinthians 15: 13–14, 17). Without the Resurrection, we would have no hope, either in this life nor in the life to come. Christ's Resurrection is the pivotal tenet of Christianity.

An extra-biblical, reliable authority concerning the Resurrection is Flavius Josephus. Josephus was a Jewish historian from Jerusalem, who was born around A.D. 33. In his account, Josephus notes:

WHEN LOVE CONQUERED ALL

Now there was about this time Jesus, a wise man, if it be lawful to call him a man; for he was a doer of wonderful works, a teacher of such men as receive the truth with pleasure. He drew over to him both many of the Jews and many of the Gentiles. He was [the] Christ. And when Pilate, at the suggestion of the principal men amongst us, had condemned him to the cross, those that loved him at the first did not forsake him; for he appeared to them alive again the third day; as the divine prophets had foretold these and ten thousand other wonderful things concerning him. And the tribe of Christians, so named from him, are not extinct at this day.

He Lives

I serve a risen Savior, He's in the world today;
I know that He is living, whatever men may say;
I see His hand of mercy, I hear his voice of cheer,
And just the time I need Him He's always near.

In all the world around me I see His loving care,
And tho' my heart grows weary I never will despair;
I know that He is leading thro' all the stormy blast,
The day of His appearing will come at last.

Rejoice, rejoice, O Christian, lift up your voice and sing
Eternal hallelujahs to Jesus Christ the King!
The Hope of all who seek Him, the Help of all who find,
None other is so loving, so good and kind.

CHORUS
He lives, He lives, Christ Jesus lives today! He walks with me
and talks with me along life's narrow way. He lives, He lives,
salvation to impart! You ask me how I know He lives?
He lives within my heart.

—A. H. Ackley

WHEN LOVE CONQUERED ALL

Blessed be the God and Father
of our Lord Jesus Christ,
which according to his abundant mercy
hath begotten us again unto a lively hope
by the resurrection of Jesus Christ from the dead,
To an inheritance incorruptible, and undefiled,
and that fadeth not away, reserved in heaven for you,
Who are kept by the power of God
through faith unto salvation ready to be revealed
in the last time.

1 Peter 1:3–8

We've prepared for, meditated upon, and celebrated this most meaningful season. Now, before we part, I extend my hand to you and with joyous conviction declare, "He is risen." By faith, I feel the warmth of your handclasp and hear your radiant reply, "He is risen, indeed!"

Sense the awe. Anticipate the hope. Experience the joy.